Advancing Through Analogies

Written by Lynne Chatham

Routledge
Taylor & Francis Group

NEW YORK AND LONDON

Illustrated by Mary Lou Johnson

First published in 2005 by Prufrock Press Inc.

Published 2021 by Routledge
605 Third Avenue, New York, NY 10017
2 Park Square, Milton Park, Abingdon, Oxon OX14 4RN

Routledge is an imprint of the Taylor & Francis Group, an informa business

Copyright © 2005 by Taylor & Francis Group

ISBN 13: 978-1-5936-3043-0 (pbk)

DOI: 10.4324/9781003232919

About This Book

What Is an Analogy?

An analogy is a comparison between two things. It points out the similarities or likenesses between things that might be different in all other respects. Analogies draw a parallel between the common characteristics of two things and cause us to think analytically about forms, usages, structures, and relationships.

Analogies are presented in the form A : B :: C : D. This relationship can be read *A is to B as C is to D*. One of these terms will be missing, and students will be asked to supply the missing term that will best complete the relationship. In the beginning stages of teaching analogical thinking, students are always presented with the standard format described above. There are, however, several acceptable analogy forms, and some of these forms are presented in this book. The possible forms for each relationship are:

A : B :: C : D	cat : meow :: dog : bark
A : C :: B : D	cat : dog :: meow : bark
B : A :: D : C	meow : cat :: bark : dog
B : D :: A : B	meow : bark :: cat : dog

Types of Analogies

Advancing Through Analogies introduces several different types of analogies. These different types are as follows:

- **Synonyms** - This analogy pairs words that have similar meanings, like *calm : serene*
- **Antonyms** - This analogy pairs words that have opposite meanings, like *cold : hot*.
- **Cause-Effect** - In this analogy, one element will cause the other thing to happen, like *fire : smoke*.
- **Part to Whole** - In this relationship, one member is an example or a part of a larger set. An example is *ring : jewelry*.
- **Part to Part** - This type of analogy pairs two members of the same set. For example, *hat: gloves* (both are articles of clothing).
- **Purpose or Use** - The words in this type of analogy express a relationship in which one word defines a purpose or use for the other word. Examples might be *pectin : jelly* (pectin is used to solidify jelly) or *bat : ball* (a bat is used to hit a ball).
- **Place or Location** - These analogies link something with its location or surrounding geographical features. Examples would be *Peru : South America* or *book : library*.

- **Association** - This type of analogy points out a relationship between words that are commonly thought to go together like *circulation : blood* and *bread : butter*.
- **Action to Object** - In these analogies, one word expresses either an action that can be preformed by or on the other word. The analogy can be written with either the action first or second. Examples are *drive : car* or *scissors : cut*.
- **Sequence or Time** - These analogies show a sequence or a development through time. Examples are *horse and carriage : automobile, evening : night* or *ABC : DEF*.
- **Characteristic or Description** - These analogies link a word with another word that is descriptive. Examples are *large : mansion* or *hero : brave*.
- **Degree** - These analogies show a continuum, usually going from lesser to greater or vice versa. Examples would be *warm : hot* or *anger : rage*.
- **Measurement** - These analogies either show the relationship between units of measure (*centimeter : meter*) or between an instrument of measure and the thing it measures (*speedometer : speed*).
- **Grammatical** - These analogies involve grammatical relationships showing tense (*do : did*), plurals (*glass : glasses*), possession (*child : child's*), or word derivation (*reverse : reversal*).
- **Mathematical** - Analogies of this type show a relationship between numbers (*1/4 : .25*) or geometry (*square : cube*).
- **Nonsemantic** - The terms in these analogies are not related by meaning but may be related by sound (*hole : whole*) or letter arrangement (*live : evil*)

Solving Analogies

The first step in solving an analogy is to look at the first pair of words and determine what relationship exists between those two words. Once a relationship has been established, the next step is to apply that relationship to the second part of the analogy and find the missing word that makes a pair of words with a similar relationship. This second step includes an initial elimination of the obviously incorrect answers and, if necessary, redefining the initial relationship if no answer completes the relationship. The entire process requires both creative and analytical thinking.

Contents

Name _____

synonym	infant : baby :: adult : grown-up
	continent : mainland :: island : isle
antonym	hard : soft :: wet : dry
	rigid : pliable :: excellent : inferior

1. **serene : tranquil :: vivacious :** _____ (a. dirty b. lively c. visible   d. cheerleader)

2. **overt : covert :: generous :** _____ (a. money b. unselfish c. philanthropist d. miserly)

3. **originality : creativity :: cordiality :** _____ (a. friendliness b. cordial c. prudish d. aloof)

4. **bold : cowardly :: invigorating :** _____ (a. exercise b. energetic c. tedious d. isometric)

5. **luxurious : plain :: rejuvenation :** _____ (a. demolition b. restore c. youth d. generous)

6. **radical : moderate :: majority :** _____ (a. most b. preponderance c. votes d. minority)

7. **bend : sag :: sanitize :** _____ (a. hospital b. clean c. dirty d. healthy)

8. **determined : obstinate :: moody :** _____ (a. mood b. gleeful c. morose d. tragedy)

9. **rough : smooth :: small :** _____ (a. granular b. person c. diminutive d. monumental)

10. **melancholy : jubilant :: pretentious :** _____ (a. haughty b. humble c. action d. doleful)

11. **ban : prohibit :: element :** _____ (a. component b. chemistry c. whole d. iron)

12. **integration : segregation :: immortality :** _____ (a. life b. mortal c. death d. people)

13. **crude : coarse :: grace :** _____ (a. movement b. refinement c. accident d. graceful)

14. **nervous : calm :: infantile :** _____ (a. puberty b. child c. disposition d. mature)

15. **goodness : decency :: evil :** _____ (a. depravity b. monster c. virtuous d. villain)

Name _____

action - object	write : book :: compose : song
	peel : banana :: crack : nut
object - action	bell : ring :: horn : honk
	play : rehearse :: game : practice

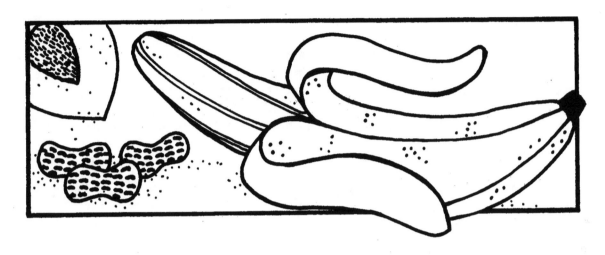

1. **concert : hear :: drama :** _____ (a. eyes b. view c. play d. spectator)

2. **maneuver : troops :: dispatch :** _____ (a. messenger b. send off c. receive d. speed)

3. **sculpt : clay :: manufacture :** _____ (a. factory b. manifest c. assemble d. products)

4. **inaugurate : officer :: enthrone :** _____ (a. office b. royalty c. throne d. commence)

5. **study : exam :: pack :** _____ (a. test b. unpack c. vacation d. package)

6. **preserve : environment :: safeguard :** _____ (a. guard b. protect c. rights d. safe)

7. **fold : origami :: slice :** _____ (a. knife b. pare c. thinly d. cheese)

8. **repress : revolution :: foster :** _____ (a. patriotism b. encourage c. fossil d. tarnish)

9. **salute : flag :: pedal :** _____ (a. flutter b. bicycle c. wares d. brake)

10. **meet : deadline :: forego :** _____ (a. abstain b. meeting c. forewarn d. temptation)

11. **solve : problem :: record :** _____ (a. round b. write down c. history d. scribe)

12. **evidence : weigh :: decision :** _____ (a. decisive b. option c. judgement d. reach)

13. **pencil : sharpen :: garbage :** _____ (a. stinky b. recycle c. trash d. truck)

14. **write : pencil :: paint :** _____ (a. brush b. picture c. artist d. landscape)

15. **throw : ceramics :: weave :** _____ (a. mosaics b. twine c. tapestry d. loom)

Name_____

synonym	great : magnificent :: melancholy : dejected
antonym	masculine : feminine :: singular : plural
object - action	prism : refract :: mirror : reflect
action - object	stroke : fire :: fasten : latch

1. **cell : divide :: seed : ____** (a. seedling b. germinate c. forest d. embryo)

2. **amateur : professional :: fiction : ____** (a. books b. story c. whimsy d. nonfiction)

3. **protect : safeguard :: hasten : ____** (a. expedite b. quickly c. move d. hinder)

4. **optional : mandatory :: manual : ____** (a. instructions b. hand c. mechanized d. small book)

5. **model : clothes :: demonstrate : ____** (a. fashion b. procedure c. illustrate d. demonstration)

6. **hyperbole : exaggeration :: brevity : ____** (a. conciseness b. brief c. speech d. duration)

7. **view : scene :: hear : ____** (a. heard b. ear c. perceptible d. sound)

8. **ostentatious : pretentious :: lethargic : ____** (a. energetic b. attitude c. listless
                                                                      d. concise)

9. **periodic : intermittent :: constant : ____** (a. changeable b. incessant c. interruption
                                                                      d. memorable)

10. **vertical : horizontal :: anterior : ____** (a. posterior b. interior c. front d. age)

11. **alteration : clothing :: revision : ____** (a. rewrite b. sight c. version d. manuscript)

12. **dearth : scarcity :: abundance : ____** (a. material b. quantity c. excess d. charity)

13. **rain : falls :: wind : ____** (a. storm b. blows c. tornado d. windy)

14. **falsehood : truth : celebrity : ____** (a. obscurity b. movie star c. fame d. notability)

15. **flutter : flag :: cut : ____** (a. bleed b. pierce c. meat d. scissors)

Name _____

cause - effect	cut : bleed :: itch : scratch
	clouds : rain :: sun : warmth
association	horse : rodeo :: elephant : circus
	pencil : paper :: paint : brush

1. **surgeon : scalpel :: bullfighter :** _____ (a. bull b. cape c. ring d. matador)

2. **winter : snow :: summer :** _____ (a. sweltering b. spring c. sun d. school)

3. **choreographer : dance :: composer :** _____ (a. music b. player c. occupation d. talent)

4. **winning : jubilation :: losing:** _____ (a. score b. game c. loser d. disappointment)

5. **marriage : union :: divorce :** _____ (a. separation b. unfortunate c. husband d. court)

6. **martial : war :: pacific :** _____ (a. Atlantic b. peace c. water d. pacify)

7. **psychology : mind :: pathology :** _____ (a. roads b. study c. disease d. religion)

8. **practice : mastery :: education :** _____ (a. student b. school c. knowledge d. facts)

9. **omnipresence : location :: omniscient :** _____ (a. grand b. knowledge c. everywhere d. wise)

10. **ultrasonic : sound :: ultraviolet :** _____ (a. purple b. light c. prism d. lightning)

11. **cold : ice :: heat :** _____ (a. steam b. hot c. heater d. temperature)

12. **guilt : conviction :: innocence :** _____ (a. morals b. children c. trial d. vindication)

13. **sadness : tears :: happiness :** _____ (a. elated b. fortuity c. smile d. melancholy)

14. **starvation : food :: suffocation :** _____ (a. death b. air c. depravation d. strangulation)

15. **recklessness : error :: war :** _____ (a. peace b. battle c. destruction d. truce)

Name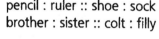

part to whole	lead : pencil :: string : guitar
	toe : foot :: finger : hand
part to part	pencil : ruler :: shoe : sock
	brother : sister :: colt : filly

1. **sole : shoe :: zipper :** _____ (a. zip b. velcro c. fastener d. coat)

2. **eraser : pencil :: tire :** _____ (a. round b. transportation c. wheel d. rubber)

3. **ring : necklace :: skirt :** _____ (a. clothing b. blouse c. pleated d. wearable)

4. **leaf : plant :: beak :** _____ (a. bird b. break c. eat d. pointed)

5. **stamp : envelope :: film :** _____ (a. strip b. negative c. camera d. flimsy)

6. **pancake : waffle :: rosemary :** _____ (a. girl b. thyme c. herb d. fragrant)

7. **palomino : Appaloosa :: Andes :** _____ (a. Appalachian b. mountain c. forested
                                                        d. South America)

8. **coral : reef :: glass :** _____ (a. silica b. transparent c. looking d. mirror)

9. **inch : foot :: ounce :** _____ (a. dram b. pound c. liter d. weight)

10. **sill : window :: bumper :** _____ (a. automobile b. hood c. protective d. collide)

11. **ostrich : penguin :: moth :** _____ (a. insect b. spider c. butterfly d. nocturnal)

12. **hemlock : pine :: limerick :** _____ (a. rhyming b. sonnet c. poem d. anthology)

13. **shell : egg :: husk :** _____ (a. corn b. husky c. covering d. pod)

14. **cumulus : cirrus :: coffee :** _____ (a. drink b. bean c. South America d. cocoa)

15. **eulogy : funeral :: valedictory :** _____ (a. speech b. solemn c. graduation d. valedictorian)

8

Name _____

cause - effect	work : income :: commerce : profit
association	decimal : ten :: binary : two
part to part	nephew : niece :: aunt : uncle
part to whole	step : staircase :: rung : ladder

1. **pennant : banner :: memo :** ____ (a. information b. paper c. notice d. succinct)

2. **ingredient : recipe :: cell :** ____ (a. organism b. cellophane c. microscopic d. cytoplasm)

3. **triangle : square :: pyramid :** ____ (a. tomb b. geometric c. 3-dimensional d. cube)

4. **lawyer : jury :: thespian :** ____ (a. actor b. audience c. drama d. mime)

5. **famine : food :: drought :** ____ (a. water b. arid c. weather d. scarcity)

6. **foot : inch :: meter :** ____ (a. metric b. centiliter c. centimeter d. linear)

7. **good fortune : happiness :: injury :** ____ (a. pain b. good health c. careless d. antiseptic)

8. **cover : book :: epidermis :** ____ (a. dermis b. covering c. skin d. body)

9. **landscape : still life :: comedy :** ____ (a. ludicrous b. comedian c. mystery d. laughter)

10. **monotony : boredom :: amusement :** ____ (a. carnival b. enjoyment c. tedium
                                                    d. pleasurable)

11. **democracy : people :: monarchy :** ____ (a. oligarchy b. butterfly c. king d. government)

12. **computer : programmer :: sextant :** ____ (a. instrument b. astronomical c. six d. navigator)

13. **hydrogen : water :: sodium :** ____ (a. salt b. chemistry c. chloride d. element)

14. **love : marriage :: faith :** ____ (a. religion b. hope c. loyalty d. obedient)

15. **Pacific : ocean :: Jupiter :** ____ (a. Uranus b. largest c. satellites d. planet)

Name_____

1. **decathlon : triathlon :: circus :** _____ (a. horses b. entertaining c. whimsical d. carnival)

2. **armada : ships :: infantry :** _____ (a. warfare b. soldiers c. munitions d. naval)

3. **bear : hibernate :: bird :** _____ (a. robin b. migrate c. food chain d. nest)

4. **water : irrigate :: air :** _____ (a. ventilate b. oxygen c. suffocation d. ozone)

5. **catastrophe : good fortune :: affluence :** _____ (a. sumptuousness b. money c. poverty d. assets)

6. **prism : spectrum :: barrier :** _____ (a. levee b. aperture c. obstruction d. shadow)

7. **metamorphosis : change :: factor :** _____ (a. divisor b. multiplication c. division d. factory)

8. **classroom : students :: menagerie :** _____ (a. zoo b. carnival c. animals d. spectator)

9. **hemoglobin : red :: chlorophyll :** _____ (a. photosynthesis b. plants c. green d. carbohydrates)

10. **virus : disease :: convalescence :** _____ (a. hospital b. rest c. doctor d. recovery)

11. **emancipate : enslave :: corrupt :** _____ (a. scrupulous b. criminal c. fraud d. offensive)

12. **Shakespeare : Hamlet :: Cervantes :** _____ (a. Spain b. author c. opera d. Don Quixote)

13. **read : map :: travel :** _____ (a. vacation b. route c. car d. tourist)

14. **stallion : mare :: boar :** _____ (a. farm b. bacon c. swine d. sow)

15. **address : concerns :: appease :** _____ (a. placate b. inflame c. complaints d. peace)

16. **calculus : trigonometry :: tennis :** _____ (a. court b. chess c. racquet d. volleyball)

17. **Louvre : Guggenheim :: St. Peter's :** _____ (a. cathedral b. Westminster c. Catholic d. Italy)

18. **memento : reminder :: pollution :** _____ (a. contamination b. ecology c. ozone d. recycle)

© Taylor & Francis • *Advancing Through Analogies*

Name _____

The analogies in this lesson are in different forms. Look at each analogy carefully. Determine the initial relationship and then find an answer that best completes that relationship.

1. **Malaysia : Iceland :: peninsula : ____** (a. tropic b. landform c. island d. ocean)

2. **strident : piercing :: enunciate : ____** (a. muffle b. pronounce c. speech d. clearly)

3. **halcyon : turbulent :: evasive : ____** (a. candid b. evasion c. elusive d. comment)

4. **understanding : communication :: discovery : ____** (a. treasure b. explorer c. scientist d. exploration)

5. **brim : hat :: cuff : ____** (a. shoe b. sleeve c. button d. hit)

6. **ballet : tap :: rock and roll : ____** (a. music b. classical c. dance d. lively)

7. **frame : membrane :: picture : ____** (a. cell b. covering c. nucleus d. portrait)

8. **preside : judge :: reign : ____** (a. precipitation b. rule c. king d. castle)

9. **Siamese : feline :: spaniel : ____** (a. poodle b. loyal c. pedigree d. canine)

10. **sun : star :: moon : ____** (a. light b. satellite c. orbiting d. planetary)

11. **overture : preface :: opera : ____** (a. book b. beginning c. table of contents d. author)

12. **Asia : Africa :: Gobi : ____** (a. arid b. desert c. Sahara d. mountain)

13. **wood : decay :: iron : ____** (a. element b. rust c. carbon d. tools)

14. **comedy : laughter :: tragedy : ____** (a. unhappy b. drama c. Hamlet d. tears)

15. **temporary : everlasting :: terminable : ____** (a. infinite b. cessation c. cancer d. career)

16. **currency : cash :: dirigible : ____** (a. transportation b. rocket c. zeppelin d. helium)

Name _____

place or location	monkey : jungle :: cow : barnyard
	ring : finger :: earring : ear
sequence or time relationship	Monday : Tuesday :: January : February
	tadpole : frog :: puppy : dog

---

1. **bird : nest :: spider :** ____ (a. ant b. web c. menacing d. arachnophobia)

2. **past : present :: yesterday :** ____ (a. time b. yesteryear c. recent d. today)

3. **abacus : calculator :: telegraph :** ____ (a. FAX b. megaphone c. electricity d. Morse Code)

4. **Greenland : Arctic :: Hawaii :** ____ (a. islands b. Honolulu c. tropical d. Pacific)

5. **Amazon : South America :: Nile :** ____ (a. Europe b. Africa c. river d. equator)

6. **graffiti : wall :: petroglyph :** ____ (a. drawing b. ancient c. symbolic d. rock)

7. **judge : court :: warden :** ____ (a. prison b. guard c. inmates d. defender)

8. **iris : eye :: cochlea :** ____ (a. anatomy b. bone c. ear d. ossicle)

9. **sextuple : septuple :: first :** ____ (a. seven b. second c. numeral d. premier)

10. **manuscript : book :: blueprint :** ____ (a. architect b. preliminary c. photographic d. building)

11. **rabbi : temple :: surgeon :** ____ (a. hospital b. physician c. scalpel d. anesthesia)

12. **AB : EF :: MN :** ____ (a. OP b. QR c. RQ d. KL)

13. **prince : king :: understudy :** ____ (a. director b. stage c. leading lady d. substitute)

14. **elementary : junior high :: freshman :** ____ (a. student b. underclassman c. school d. senior)

15. **fledgling : bird :: bud :** ____ (a. blooming b. sprouting c. flower d. protuberance)

Name _____

characteristic or description	hot : lava :: cold : iceberg
	fast : cheetah :: slow : snail
degree	pink : red :: gray : black
	good : great :: bad : horrible

1. **shrub : tree :: pond :** _____ (a. halcyon b. water c. lake d. river)

2. **solid : ice :: gas :** _____ (a. fluid b. gas mask c. gasoline d. steam)

3. **iridescent : opal :: glistening :** _____ (a. sparkling b. diamond c. ring d. drab)

4. **seed : plant :: egg :** _____ (a. yolk b. reproduction c. bird d. Fabergé)

5. **hill : mountain :: islet :** _____ (a. island b. ocean c. continent d. tropical)

6. **mansion : grandiose :: cottage :** _____ (a. abode b. woods c. residence d. unpretentious)

7. **ornate : decoration :: stationary :** _____ (a. stationery b. statue c. immovable d. wind-borne)

8. **talk : jabber :: walk :** _____ (a. scurry b. feet c. parade d. gait)

9. **bloodcurdling : yell :: wistful :** _____ (a. blithe b. laugh c. sigh d. introspective)

10. **octagon : nonagon :: million :** _____ (a. thousand b. billion c. numeral d. millionaire)

11. **path : road :: stream :** _____ (a. river b. rippling c. brook d. current)

12. **sanitary : hospital :: thought-provoking :** _____ (a. thinking b. monotonous c. stimulating
d. classroom)

13. **storm : hurricane :: rule :** _____ (a. obey b. classroom c. law d. judge)

14. **explosive : fireworks :: complicated :** _____ (a. Fourth of July b. labyrinth c. difficult d. facile)

15. **hysterical : scream :: muffled :** _____ (a. whisper b. muffler c. mute d. sonorous)

Name _____

place or location	bank : money :: photographs : album
characteristic or description	ruby : red :: sapphire : blue
sequence or time	past : present :: yesterday : today
degree or hierarchy	possible : probable :: similar : identical

1. **snack : meal :: party :** ____ (a. festival b. edibles c. gathering d. convivial)

2. **buoyant : cork :: iridescent :** ____ (a. lackluster b. iridium c. bubble d. iris)

3. **gun : cannon :: skiff :** ____ (a. moorage b. yacht c. sail d. seaworthy)

4. **arch : doorway :: bridge :** ____ (a. girders b. automobile c. suspension d. valley)

5. **limousine : automobile :: manor :** ____ (a. house b. mansion c. mammoth d. estate)

6. **grape : wine :: wheat :** ____ (a. flour b. grain c. barley d. harvest)

7. **audible : sound :: visible :** ____ (a. visual b. sight c. perceivable d. overlook)

8. **admiral : sea :: general :** ____ (a. army b. commander c. lieutenant d. land)

9. **snicker : laugh :: whimper :** ____ (a. inconsolable b. cry c. ludicrous d. whine)

10. **week : month :: month :** ____ (a. day b. calendar c. year d. bimonthly)

11. **intern : physician :: apprentice :** ____ (a. craftsman b. trade c. student d. learning)

12. **faculty : university :: jury :** ____ (a. court b. judge c. criminal d. lawyer)

13. **gourmet : food :: connoisseur :** ____ (a. authority b. critical c. athletics d. art)

14. **telegraph : telephone :: radio :** ____ (a. waves b. auditory c. television d. wireless)

15. **Andes : South America :: Rocky :** ____ (a. mountain b. North America c. precipitous
                                 d. Colorado)

Name _____

| measurement | thermometer : temperature :: speedometer : speed
clock : time :: odometer : distance |
| grammatical | child : children :: man : men
see : saw :: do : did |

1. **disqualification : disqualify :: legislation :** ____ (a. congress b. mandate c. laws d. legislate)

2. **bad : worst :: good :** ____ (a. better b. worse c. best d. okay)

3. **ampere : electricity :: candela :** ____ (a. light b. candle c. illuminate d. optics)

4. **udometer : rain :: barometer :** ____ (a. mercury b. wind c. atmospheric pressure
                                                      d. barogram)

5. **altimeter : altitude :: anemometer :** ____ (a. anemograph b. rain c. speed d. wind)

6. **evolution : evolve :: idiotic :** ____ (a. idiot b. stupid c. intelligent d. idiosyncrasy)

7. **fish : fishes :: waltz :** ____ (a. dance b. waltzes c. waltzer d. ballroom)

8. **I.Q. : intelligence :: Celsius :** ____ (a. Fahrenheit b. scale c. liquids d. temperature)

9. **diary : diaries :: sky :** ____ (a. earth b. celestial c. skies d. clouds)

10. **bathometer : depth :: seismograph :** ____ (a. size b. earth movement c. intensity
                                                        d. seismology)

11. **he : she :: gander :** ____ (a. goose b. peacock c. female d. egg)

12. **foot : feet :: woman :** ____ (a. man b. women's c. women d. female)

13. **me : mine :: America :** ____ (a. American b. United States c. Amerigo Vespucci d. Mexico)

14. **analysis : analyses :: oasis :** ____ (a. desert b. oasises c. fertile d. oases)

15. **peck : bushel :: quart :** ____ (a. jar b. gallon c. pint d. quarter)

Lesson 13

Name_____

purpose: use	zoo : animals :: museum : artifacts
	sugar : sweeten :: yeast : leaven
mathematical	2 : 3 :: 7 : 8
nonsemantic	too : to :: pair : pare
	lost : lots :: past : pats

1. **antiseptic : bacteria :: fungicide : ____** (a. nutrient b. destroy c. chlorophyll d. fungi)

2. **9 : 19 :: 55 : ____** (a. 45 b. 65 c. 110 d. 75)

3. **music : listening :: art : ____** (a. exquisite b. gallery c. artist d. viewing)

4. **quills : porcupine :: armor : ____** (a. armory b. weapons c. knight d. protective)

5. **rail : lair :: lame : ____** (a. male b. crippled c. leap d. meals)

6. **2 : 5 :: 10 : ____** (a. 21 b. 20 c. 15 d. 12)

7. **insecticide : insects :: herbicide : ____** (a. herbal b. poison c. plants d. flavoring)

8. **telescope : universe :: microscope : ____** (a. microorganism b. lenses c. magnify d. biology)

9. **4 : 16 :: 13 : ____** (a. 26 b. 169 c. 51 d. 31)

10. **magician : entertain :: scientist : ____** (a. analytical b. physics c. laboratory d. investigate)

11. **5 : 26 :: 7 : ____** (a. 50 b. 49 c. 29 d. 35)

12. **peek : keep :: evil : ____** (a. life b. good c. live d. vile)

13. **heart : circulation :: lung : ____** (a. oxygen b. respiration c. anatomy d. bronchi)

14. **.25 : 1/4 :: .125 : ____** (a. 1/8 b. 1/2 c. 1/6 d. .50)

15. **mask : face :: helmet : ____** (a. head b. headpiece c. protective d. safeguard)

16

© Taylor & Francis • *Advancing Through Analogies*

Name _____

purpose or use	press : print :: eraser : efface
measurement	gram : weight :: liter : capacity
grammatical	eat : ate :: meet : met
mathematical	12 : 6 :: 50 : 25
nonsemantic	horse : hoarse :: meet : meat

1. **decibel : loudness :: decade :** ____ (a. time b. ten c. century d. decagon)

2. $2x^3 : 6x^2 :: 7y^4 :$ ____ (a. $6y^5$ b. $28y^3$ c. $14y^3$ d. $28y^2$)

3. **are : aren't :: do :** ____ (a. does b. can't c. doesn't d. don't)

4. **calorie : heat :: acre :** ____ (a. mile b. square c. land d. acre-foot)

5. **itinerary : trip :: script :** ____ (a. manuscript b. play c. director d. dialogue)

6. **levee : water :: muzzle :** ____ (a. restraint b. leather c. mutter d. biting)

7. **rise : rose :: go :** ____ (a. went b. goes c. come d. gone)

8. **radius : 3 :: diameter :** ____ (a. 6 b. circle c. 9 d. geometry)

9. **photometer : light :: audiometer :** ____ (a. VCR b. sound c. magnetic d. radio)

10. **billboard : advertise :: credential :** ____ (a. credible b. teacher c. authorize d. document)

11. **skin : body :: case :** ____ (a. container b. enclose c. internal d. machinery)

12. **ox : oxen :: deer :** ____ (a. deer b. elk c. mammal d. ruminant)

13. **complementary : 90 :: supplementary :** ____ (a. angle b. 180 c. additional d. 45)

14. **better : best :: longer :** ____ (a. short b. long c. space d. longest)

15. **knot : speed :: league :** ____ (a. ocean b. baseball c. distance d. nations)

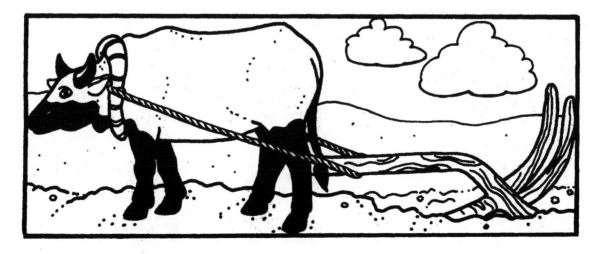

Name_____

1. **board foot : lumber :: carat :** _____ (a. carrot b. measurement c. gold d. liquids)

2. **leaf : leaves :: octopus :** _____ (a. ocean b. squid c. tentacles d. octopi)

3. **embarrassed : mortified :: tepid :** _____ (a. water b. temperature c. torrid d. frosty)

4. **philanthropy : humanitarian :: massacre :** _____ (a. barbarous b. bloodshed c. suicide d. gentle)

5. **golf : course :: hockey :** _____ (a. puck b. league c. rink d. perilous)

6. **4/5 : 5/4 :: 2/3 :** _____ (a. .66 b. 1 2/3 c. 4/6 d. 3/2)

7. **meter : distance :: liter :** _____ (a. milliliter b. water c. capacity d. gallon)

8. **gills: fish :: lungs :** _____ (a. respiratory b. humans c. breathe d. oxygen)

9. **larva : pupa :: sapling :** _____ (a. tree b. sap c. maple syrup d. sapphire)

10. **daughter : mother :: niece :** _____ (a. nephew b. aunt c. cousin d. relative)

11. **exercise : gymnasium :: eat :** _____ (a. sustenance b. ingest c. obesity d. cafeteria)

12. **lay : lies :: do :** _____ (a. doing b. did c. don't d. does)

13. **pharaoh : Egypt :: monk :** _____ (a. monastery b. religious c. brother d. cloistered)

14. **fable : fictitious :: ballad :** _____ (a. song b. folk c. melodious d. balladeer)

15. **confusion : pandemonium :: skirmish :** _____ (a. offensive b. frolic c. truce d. battle)

16. **5 : 14 :: 20 :** _____ (a. 29 b. 61 c. 39 d. 43)

17. **descendant : ancestor :: children :** _____ (a. child b. school c. parent d. immature)

18. **whole : hole :: not :** _____ (a. negative b. knot c. nothing d. note)

Name _____

The analogies in this lesson are in different forms. Look at each analogy carefully. Determine the initial relationship and then find an answer that best completes that relationship.

1. **geriatrics : old age :: pediatrics :** _____ (a. medicine b. infancy c. doctor d. illness)

2. **1/2 : 1/4 :: .52 :** _____ (a. .26 b. 1.04 c. .50 d. 26/50)

3. **more difficult : difficult :: easier :** _____ (a. complex b. easiest c. facile d. easy)

4. **teaspoon : tablespoon :: dram :** _____ (a. liter b. pound c. ounce d. quart)

5. **request : plead :: examine :** _____ (a. science b. scrutinize c. divulge d. examination)

6. **massive : mountain :: arid :** _____ (a. desert b. dry c. river bed d. moist)

7. **pupil : teacher :: teacher :** _____ (a. instructor b. compassionate c. classroom d. principal)

8. **duet : solo :: dialogue :** _____ (a. conversion b. speech c. monologue d. drama)

9. **tennis : hockey :: racquet :** _____ (a. ice b. stick c. court d. mallet)

10. **millimeter : centimeter :: liter :** _____ (a. dekaliter b. centiliter c. quart d. measurement)

11. **hammer : carpenter :: press :** _____ (a. ink b. compress c. paper d. printer)

12. **6 : 110 :: decimal :** _____ (a. binary b. quinary c. multiplication d. two)

13. **senior : junior :: toddler :** _____ (a. child b. parent c. infant d. curious)

14. **yellow : cowardly :: white :** _____ (a. color b. pure c. black d. bride)

15. **anger : rage :: happiness :** _____ (a. party b. sorrowful c. clown d. ecstasy)

Name_____

1. **stagnant : pond :: ____ : pasture** (a. cows b. farm c. bucolic d. lake)

2. **____ : hovercraft :: dirigible : helicopter** (a. steamship b. airplane c. float d. rapid)

3. **scale : cliff :: ____ : river** (a. flows b. bank c. meandering d. ford)

4. **stop : ____ :: tool : loot** (a. tops b. pots c. go d. stool)

5. **adhesive : bonding :: solvent : ____** (a. turpentine b. glue c. dissolving d. noxious)

6. **goes : go :: ____ : are** (a. is b. went c. am d. were)

7. **____ : millimeter :: pound : kilogram** (a. weight b. height c. meter d. inch)

8. **igneous : ____ :: hurricane : cyclone** (a. rock b. volcano c. weather d. metamorphic)

9. **lobby : hotel :: ____ : church** (a. synagogue b. sanctuary c. sacred d. worship)

10. **protagonist : hero :: antagonist : ____** (a. villain b. fiction c. heroine d. author)

11. **____ : earth :: celestial : heaven** (a. world b. planet c. terrestrial d. Mars)

12. **Italy : Mediterranean :: ____ : Caribbean** (a. Australia b. sea c. tropical d. Mexico)

13. **____ : addition :: one : multiplication** (a. subtraction b. zero c. one d. addend)

14. **smile : chuckle :: ____ : sob** (a. sadness b. snicker c. weep d. tantrum)

15. **hypnotist : ____ :: clown : amuse** (a. mesmerize b. magician c. therapist d. spellbinding)

16. **food : famine :: cleanliness : ____** (a. sanitation b. white c. immaculate d. squalor)

17. **Cantonese : China :: Hindi : ____** (a. Hindu b. India c. Pakistani d. language)

18. **____ : heat :: current : water** (a. blistering b. cold c. convection d. summer)

Name _____

1. **pear : _____ :: their : there** (a. fruit b. pair c. tree d. they're)

2. **_____ : 8 :: 56 : 7** (a. 15 b. 78 c. 64 d. 71)

3. **short story : _____ :: fable : saga** (a. plot b. anecdote c. novel d. novelist)

4. **espionage : clandestine :: diplomacy : _____** (a. cooperative b. embassy c. governments d. truce)

5. **flora : _____ :: fauna : animals** (a. Latin b. plants c. birds d. butterflies)

6. **_____ : weapons :: closet : clothes** (a. defense b. guns c. destructive d. armory)

7. **examination : knowledge :: _____ : finances** (a. business b. financial c. audit d. money)

8. **mosque : cathedral :: pyramid : _____** (a. catacombs b. Egypt c. sphinx d. colossal)

9. **heat : evaporation :: _____ : condensation** (a. vapor b. enlarge c. rain d. cooling)

10. **_____ : warring :: respectful : insolent** (a. battle b. peaceful c. commander d. hostile)

11. **renaissance : _____ :: frontier : boundary** (a. Dark Ages b. da Vinci c. revival d. Italy)

12. **child : children :: company : _____** (a. business b. company's c. companies' d. companies)

13. **protractor : _____ :: ruler : length** (a. angles b. compass c. sound d. mathematics)

14. **_____ : light bulb :: sundial : clock** (a. light b. candle c. electricity d. lumina)

15. **texture : _____ :: color : visual** (a. cloth b. rough c. tactile d. auditory)

16. **decipher : code :: solve : _____** (a. solution b. pensive c. detective d. puzzle)

17. **storm : rain :: _____ : snow** (a. flake b. condensation c. frozen d. blizzard)

18. **_____ : space :: acoustics : sound** (a. geometry b. universe c. outer d. pathology)

Name_____

1. **constitution : ____ :: scrapbook : mementos** (a. government b. lasting c. rules d. frivolous)

2. **____ : morals :: genetics : heredity** (a. personal b. moralist c. conduct d. ethics)

3. **instinct : behavior :: heredity : ____** (a. parentage b. Darwin c. knowledge d. physical traits)

4. **mandatory : ____ :: juvenile : mature** (a. compulsory b. voluntary c. taxes d. command)

5. **nightmare : dream :: storm : ____** (a. precipitation b. night c. menacing d. winter)

6. **herbivore : cow :: carnivore : ____** (a. plants b. omnivore c. lion d. vegetarian)

7. **mutiny : rebellion :: ____ : pact** (a. dispute b. treaty c. signature d. written)

8. **hydroelectric : nuclear :: solar : ____** (a. sun b. energy c. panel d. wind)

9. **magnet : attract :: pendulum : ____** (a. vacillate b. clock c. string d. arc)

10. **____ : .75 :: .83 : .23** (a. .15 b. 1.35 c. .81 d. .69)

11. **earn : respect :: ____ : ridicule** (a. bad feelings b. sarcasm c. avoid d. ridiculous)

12. **____ : sparkling :: lethargic : lifeless** (a. ebullient b. diamond c. drab d. shine)

13. **translucent : transparent :: powerful : ____** (a. weak b. hurricane c. opaque
                                              d. omnipotent)

14. **anatomy : ____ :: physiology : function** (a. science b. composition c. biology d. doctor)

15. **fresco : art :: ____ : music** (a. scherzo b. orchestra c. notes d. musician)

16. **exclusive : unrestrictive :: perfect : ____** (a. impeccable b. appearance c. flawed d. behavior)

17. **____ : light :: microwave : electromagnet** (a. luminous b. optics c. darkness d. laser)

18. **author : originate :: ____ : replicate** (a. copy b. plagiarist c. information d. publication)

Name _____

1. **geodesic : ____ :: Corinthian : column** (a. geometry b. triangle c. dome d. curved)

2. **ceremony : ritual :: ____ : commemoration** (a. holiday b. birthday card c. pleasurable
     d. vacation)

3. **____ : stage :: movie : set** (a. performance b. stage c. platform d. theater)

4. **century : decade :: decameter : ____** (a. measurement b. kilometer c. meter d. yard)

5. **galaxy : star :: ____ : building** (a. house b. windows c. metropolis d. domicile)

6. **latitude : longitude :: clock : ____** (a. calendar b. time c. grandfather d. epoch)

7. **____ : environment :: paleontology : fossils** (a. study b. ecology c. pollution d. stratosphere)

8. **player : ____ :: singer : chorus** (a. cooperative b. coach c. competitor d. team)

9. **abdicate : throne :: resign : ____** (a. relinquish b. continue c. office d. design)

10. **vigilantism : lawlessness :: ____ : dictator** (a. autocrat b. subjects c. government
      d. bureaucrat)

11. **xylem : ____ :: artery : blood** (a. plants b. botany c. leaves d. water)

12. **____ : clock :: alchemy : chemistry** (a. quartz b. hourglass c. watch d. chronology)

13. **refraction : bending :: friction : ____** (a. rubbing b. fiction c. fraction d. heat)

14. **____ : predator :: colleague : associate** (a. parasite b. prey c. symbiosis d. host)

15. **colosseum : sports :: academy : ____** (a. school b. audience c. education d. scholarly)

16. **____ : heterogeneous :: antiquated : ultramodern** (a. archaic b. homogeneous
      c. miscellaneous d. components)

17. **FORTRAN : computer :: ____ : medicine** (a. Latin b. hospital c. doctor d. insurance)

18. **griffin : ____ :: Paul Bunyan : Johnny Appleseed** (a. magical b. fictional c. chimera
      d. fearsome)

Name_____

1. **refugee : ____ :: detective : evidence** (a. safety b. country c. fugitive d. immigrate)

2. **elastic : stretch :: magnet : ____** (a. poles b. field c. iron d. attract)

3. **49 : 7 :: ____ : 10** (a. 60 b. 100 c. 120 d. 17)

4. **____ : comedy :: serious : frivolous** (a. humorous b. comedian c. tragedy d. snicker)

5. **alcohol : intoxication :: ____ : sobriety** (a. teetotaler b. abstinence c. drink d. inebriate)

6. **____ : checkers :: tennis : volleyball** (a. backgammon b. board c. player d. game)

7. **satire : slapstick :: parable : ____** (a. Aesop b. entertaining c. lesson d. allegory)

8. **teach : ____ :: write : wrote** (a. teacher b. taught c. pupil d. learn)

9. **light year : distance :: foot-candle : ____** (a. candle b. distance c. galaxy d. light)

10. **metaphysics : ____ :: hydraulics : physics** (a. philosophy b. physics c. cognition d. aesthetics)

11. **____ : constant :: limited : infinite** (a. habitual b. frequent c. occasional d. perpetual)

12. **hologram : 3-dimensional :: ____ : reflective** (a. photograph b. mirror c. absorbent
                                                      d. reflection)

13. **____ : Paleozoic :: Dark Ages : Renaissance** (a. epoch b. paleology c. Mississippian
                                                      d. Mesozoic)

14. **airplane : transportation :: telephone : ____** (a. communication b. answering machine
                                                      c. FAX d. Alexander Graham Bell)

15. **castle : ____ :: barricade : blockade** (a. royalty b. moat c. fortification d. monumental)

16. **circle : semicircle :: ____ : trapezoid** (a. geometry b. quadrilateral c. triangle d. hexagon)

17. **____ : camera :: pupil : eye** (a. cornea b. aperture c. photography d. focus)

18. **crab : shrimp :: ____ : cotton** (a. ball b. bale c. linen d. fiber)

Name _____

1. **proprietor : business :: curator : ____** (a. cloister b. administrator c. museum d. agglomerate)

2. **____ : mate :: tale : late** (a. companion b. tame c. mate's d. faithful)

3. **Mohs scale : ____ :: Richter scale : earthquake** (a. mole b. geology c. science d. hardness)

4. **ordinal : cardinal :: ____ : fifty** (a. fiftieth b. 50 c. one hundred d. five)

5. **____ : exclaim :: tattle : slander** (a. listen b. tell c. excitedly d. speaker)

6. **combustion : ____ :: condensation : moisture** (a. engine b. friction c. heat d. flammable)

7. **abbreviation : etc. :: ____ : AIDS** (a. disease b. contagious c. oxymoron d. acronym)

8. **parenthesis : parentheses :: cactus : ____** (a. grammar b. cacti c. desert d. plant)

9. **pyramid : ____ :: gymnasium : physical education** (a. tomb b. triangular c. archaic d. skyscraper)

10. **____ : jet plane :: rowboat : hydroplane** (a. aerodynamics b. pilot c. glider d. pagoda)

11. **Twain : Finn :: Dickens : ____** (a. Scrooge b. Sawyer c. fictitious d. pseudonym)

12. **molecule : ____ :: note : music** (a. atom b. matter c. chemistry d. formula)

13. **isthmus : Panama :: archipelago : ____** (a. islands b. peninsula c. Greenland d. Philippines)

14. **seize : ____ :: shun : adversity** (a. expropriate b. carpe diem c. opportunity d. relinquish)

15. **blackmail : extortion :: ____ : praise** (a. flattery b. penalty c. worthy d. achievement)

16. **oblivion : fame :: natural : ____** (a. nature b. food c. organic d. artificial)

17. **happy : ____ :: smart : genius** (a. ecstatic b. sorrowful c. clown d. contented)

18. **formal : prom :: ____ : hoe-down** (a. dance b. polka c. quiet d. exuberant)

Name_____

1. **solar : sun :: lunar :** ____ (a. lunacy b. tides c. moon d. crescent)

2. **Plato :** ____ **:: Bach : Beethoven** (a. music b. Aristotle c. planet d. Mozart)

3. **architecture : building :: agronomy :** ____ (a analysis b. animals c. agrarian d. crops)

4. **your :** ____ **:: their : theirs** (a. you b. yours c. my d. his)

5. **square : cube ::** ____ **: sphere** (a. globular b. ball c. circle d. 3-dimensional)

6. **15 : -1 :: 10 :** ____ (a. -6 b. 26 c. -5 d. 6)

7. **skeptic : questioning ::** ____ **: testifying** (a. testimonial b. disprove c. evangelist d. judge)

8. **COBOL : BASIC ::** ____ **: Italian** (a. Roman b. Mediterranean c. language d. French)

9. **scholar : school :: scientist :** ____ (a. experiment b. laboratory c. hypothesis d. empirical)

10. **input :** ____ **:: output : printer** (a. keyboard b. computer c. garbage d. information)

11. **patriot : traitor ::** ____ **: subordinate** (a. commander b. underling c. acquiesce d. perfunctory)

12. **jealousy : envy ::** ____ **: dormancy** (a. activity b. inert c. hibernation d. animated)

13. ____ **: enlightenment :: practice : improvement** (a. indifference b. luminous c. precaution d. education)

14. **pedometer : foot :: tachometer :** ____ (a. distance b. car c. speedometer d. thermometer)

15. **maximum : minimum :: imitation :** ____ (a. authentic b. flavoring c. alias d. counterfeit)

16. **incandescent :** ____ **:: fluorescent : phosphors** (a. light bulb b. illuminate c. filament d. temperature)

17. ____ **: taste :: auditory : hearing** (a. tongue b. food c. gustatory d. buds)

18. **decagon : pentagon ::** ____ **: rectangle** (a. quadrilateral b. square c. geometry d. octagon)

Name _____

1. ____ : ciphers :: detective : spy (a. secret b. codes c. symbolic d. speculate)

2. obscure : vague :: apparent : ____ (a. parent b. explanation c. obvious d. comprehend)

3. ____ : Arctic :: Buddhism : Islam (a. ocean b. circle c. frigid d. Indian)

4. quartz : ____ :: pasta : spaghetti (a. granite b. crystal c. basalt d. mineral)

5. happenstance : accident :: ____ : courage (a. hero b. valor c. chivalrous d. medal of honor)

6. pagoda : ____ :: pyramid : Egypt (a. China b. sacred c. tower d. temple)

7. ____ : penalty :: discount : price (a. foul b. violation c. commute d. punishment)

8. barbarian : civilized :: catalyst : ____ (a. impetus b. accelerate c. catharsis d. deterrent)

9. ichthyologist : fish :: ____ : animal (a. mammal b. zoologist c. botanist d. archaeology)

10. cow : herd :: ____ : gaggle (a. giggle b. practical joke c. pheasant d. goose)

11. aerodynamics : physics :: ____ : mathematics (a. science b. computations c. algebra
                                                                    d. cerebral)

12. curmudgeon : ____ :: humanitarian : charitable (a. cantankerous b. Scrooge c. crab
                                                                    d. congenial)

13. ____ : onomatopoeia :: who : interrogatory (a. poetry b. sizzle c. anagram d. haiku)

14. eccentric : bizarre :: ordinary : ____ (a. mundane b. exceptional c. responsibilities d. ordinal)

15. doctor : ____ :: lawyer : client (a. physician b. hospital c. patient d. medical)

16. ____ : documents :: silo : grain (a. chronicles b. official c. archives d. judicial)

17. palette : paint :: ____ : words (a. dictionary b. synonyms c. verb d. lexicon)

18. appetite : eat :: exhaustion : ____ (a. tiredness b. energy c. rest d. exercise)

Name_____

1. **musician : orchestra :: actor :** ____ (a. actress b. script c. director d. cast)

2. **nucleus : cell ::** ____ **: country** (a. capital b. capitol c. metropolis d. continent)

3. **exodus : arrival ::** ____ **: immigrate** (a. colonist b. immigrant c. emigrate d. expatriation)

4. **chief : tribe :: admiral :** ____ (a. fleet b. commander c. general d. officer)

5. **infantile :** ____ **:: old : ancient** (a. teenager b. juvenile c. youngster d. maturing)

6. **homogenize : milk :: amalgamate :** ____ (a. malevolence b. cheese c. merge d. companies)

7. ____ **: infamous :: objective : unbiased** (a. dignitary b. renown c. notorious d. importance)

8. **melee : riot ::** ____ **: pain** (a. discomfort b. anguish c. injury d. headache)

9. **5/6 :** ____ **:: 3/8 : 2 2/3** (a. 2 2/6 b. 1 1/5 c. 1 4/6 d. 10/12)

10. ____ **: persuasion :: slander : scandal** (a. personal b. deterrent c. hinder d. propaganda)

11. **frequency : hertz :: resistance :** ____ (a. opposition b. watt c. ohms d. electricity)

12. **galaxy : immense :: microbe :** ____ (a. minuscule b. cell c. microbiology d. microscope)

13. **glaze : pottery ::** ____ **: cell** (a. ceramics b. membrane c. nucleus d. organism)

14. **Christmas :** ____ **:: basilica : synagogue** (a. Hanukkah b. holiday c. religious d. celebration)

15. ____ **: magnifies :: lantern : illuminates** (a. enlarge b. magnitude c. diminish d. microscope)

16. **communication : ideas :: commerce :** ____ (a. commercial b. merchandising c. commodities
      d. entrepreneur)

17. **Brahms :** ____ **:: Shakespeare : Dickens** (a. musician b. lullaby c. Handel d. da Vinci)

18. ____ **: alpine :: Italy : Mediterranean** (a. Egypt b. mountainous c. Alps d. Switzerland)

Name _____

1. **hostile : pacific ::** ____ **: fragrant** (a. flower b. putrid c. perfume d. olfactory)

2. **radar :** ____ **:: bridge : span** (a. radio b. sonar c. conceal d. locate)

3. **Apache : Navajo ::** ____ **: Inca** (a. Peru b. Indian c. empire d. Maya)

4. **gorilla : primate :: gopher :** ____ (a. rodent b. garden c. mole d. subterranean)

5. ____ **: many :: monopoly : one** (a. pentameter b. polytheism c. bilingual d. quadrant)

6. **bacteria :** ____ **:: therapy : healing** (a. virus b. antiseptic c. infection d. microscope)

7. **bale : hay ::** ____ **: paper** (a. pencil b. news c. wood d. ream)

8. **hawk :** ____ **:: war : peace** (a. dove b. aggressive c. flight d. falcon)

9. **obedient : dutiful ::** ____ **: defiant** (a. compliant b. rebellious c. teenager d. mutiny)

10. **grammar : language :: computation :** ____ (a. addition b. calculate c. arithmetic
    d. numeral)

11. **plane : land :: ship :** ____ (a. dock b. water c. sailor d. vessel)

12. **ombudsman :** ____ **:: judge : justice** (a. officer b. citizens c. ombudswoman d. complaints)

13. **bacteria : bacterium ::** ____ **: criterion** (a. standard b. criteria c. judgement d. critique)

14. **4/5 :** ____ **:: 3/4 : .75** (a. .80 b. .40 c. .50 d. 1.25)

15. **sometimes : always :: sporadic :** ____ (a. spores b. unremitting c. weather d. unreliable)

16. **swear :** ____ **:: adhere to : rules** (a. affirm b. witness c. oath d. punishment)

17. ____ **: sword :: archery : arrow** (a. fencing b. sabre c. piercing d. knight)

18. **pasteurize : milk ::** ____ **: surgical instruments** (a. surgeon b. operation c. sterilize
    d. contaminate)

Name _____

1. **contaminate : pollute ::** _____ **: safeguard** (a. fence b. sentinel c. jeopardize d. protect)

2. _____ **: conifer :: octopus : mollusk** (a. deciduous b. cone c. pine d. forest)

3. **Churchill :** _____ **:: Monet : Picasso** (a. Nehru b. prime minister c. England d. diplomat)

4. **intermediate :** _____ **:: mediocre : exceptional** (a. beginning b. advanced c. medium d. level)

5. **stanza : poem ::** _____ **: play** (a. actor b. director c. scene d. movie)

6. **umbrella :** _____ **:: hat : sun** (a. rain b. protective c. beach d. parasol)

7. **baldness : hair :: deafness :** _____ (a. mute b. hearing c. hearing aid d. loud noise)

8. **exacerbate : soothe ::** _____ **: bungle** (a. mismanage b. task c. butterfingers d. manage)

9. **he : his :: man :** _____ (a. men b. men's c. man's d. woman)

10. **rhyme :** _____ **:: rhythm : beat** (a. sound b. poetry c. nursery d. jingle)

11. **link :** _____ **:: bead : necklace** (a. golf b. chain c. bond d. loop)

12. **spending : debt ::** _____ **: reserves** (a. reservation b. bank c. thrifty d. saving)

13. _____ **: meter :: pint : quart** (a. metric b. yard c. centimeter d. kilogram)

14. **launch : rocket :: kickoff :** _____ (a. campaign b. quarterback c. commence d. kickback)

15. **flag :** _____ **:: dove : peace** (a. ripple b. country c. banner d. patriotism)

16. **caffeine : arouses ::** _____ **: calms** (a. tranquil b. turbulent c. conflict d. sedative)

17. **Rodin : Tchaikovsky :: sculpture :** _____ (a. music b. art c. Strauss d. statue)

18. **baseball :** _____ **:: pool : table** (a. bat b. diamond c. uniform d. ping pong)

Name _____

1. **democracy : ____ :: aristocracy : elite** (a. electorate b. capitalism c. dictator d. freedom)

2. **cotton : natural :: polyester : ____** (a. acetate b. petroleum c. synthetic d. fiber)

3. **synonyms : ____ :: poems : anthology** (a. antonyms b. homonyms c. connotation
                                                                d. thesaurus)

4. **strike : strum :: tambourine : ____** (a. music b. guitar c. instrument d. percussion)

5. **____ : crustacean :: potato : tuber** (a. crab b. bivalve c. ocean d. delicacy)

6. **immunity : protection :: ____ : combination** (a. division b. fission c. fusion d. permutation)

7. **Cancer : Capricorn :: Arctic : ____** (a. Antarctic b. freezing c. Greenland d. North Pole)

8. **hue : ____ :: tow : toe** (a. color b. tint c. hew d. who)

9. **ocher : yellow :: ____ : purple** (a. royalty b. grapes c. turquoise d. lavender)

10. **____ : analgesic :: iodine : antiseptic** (a. remedy b. aspirin c. pain killer d. healing)

11. **taciturn : talkative :: energetic : ____** (a. sedentary b. athlete c. lively d. training)

12. **enterprise : ____ :: labor : wages** (a. business b. spaceship c. profit d. communism)

13. **sand : hourglass :: ____ : watch** (a. quartz crystal b. clock c. wrist d. timepiece)

14. **Mexico : North America :: ____ : Africa** (a. Asia b. Atlantic c. Egypt d. continent)

15. **alliteration : ____ :: collage : art** (a. hyperbole b. language c. repetitious d. metaphor)

16. **gate : fence :: ____ : mountain** (a. pass b. range c. Everest d. volcanic)

17. **hovercraft : submarine :: dermatitis : ____** (a. skin b. disease c. arthritis d. rash)

18. **chemistry : physics :: ____ : geography** (a. mathematics b. mountains c. school d. history)

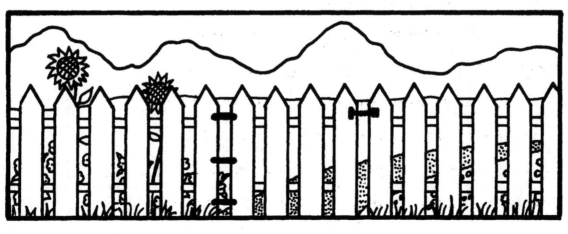

Answers

Lesson 1
1. b. lively
2. d. miserly
3. a. friendliness
4. c. tedious
5. a. demolition
6. d. minority
7. b. clean
8. c. morose
9. d. monumental
10. b. humble
11. a. component
12. c. death
13. b. refinement
14. d. mature
15. a. depravity

Lesson 2
1. b. view
2. a. messenger
3. d. products
4. b. royalty
5. c. vacation
6. c. rights
7. d. cheese
8. a. patriotism
9. b. bicycle
10. d. temptation
11. c. history
12. d. reach
13. b. recycle
14. a. brush
15. c. tapestry

Lesson 3
1. b. germinate
2. d. nonfiction
3. a. expedite
4. c. mechanized
5. b. procedure
6. a. conciseness
7. d. sound
8. c. listless
9. b. incessant
10. a. posterior
11. d. manuscript
12. c. excess
13. b. blows
14. a. obscurity
15. d. scissors

Lesson 4
1. b. cape
2. c. sun
3. a. music
4. d. disappointment
5. a. separation
6. b. peace
7. c. disease
8. c. knowledge
9. b. knowledge
10. b. light
11. a. steam
12. d. vindication
13. c. smile
14. b. air
15. c. destruction

Lesson 5
1. d. coat
2. c. wheel
3. b. blouse
4. a. bird
5. c. camera
6. b. thyme
7. a. Appalachian
8. d. mirror
9. b. pound
10. a. automobile
11. c. butterfly
12. b. sonnet
13. a. corn
14. d. cocoa
15. c. graduation

Lesson 6
1. c. notice
2. a. organism
3. d. cube
4. b. audience
5. a. water
6. c. centimeter
7. a. pain
8. d. body
9. c. mystery
10. b. enjoyment
11. c. king
12. d. navigator
13. a. salt
14. a. religion
15. d. planet

Lesson 7
1. d. carnival
2. b. soldiers
3. b. migrate
4. a. ventilate
5. c. poverty
6. d. shadow
7. a. divisor
8. c. animals
9. c. green
10. d. recovery
11. a. scrupulous
12. d. Don Quixote
13. b. route
14. d. sow
15. c. complaints
16. d. volleyball
17. b. Westminster
18. a. contamination

Lesson 8
1. c. island
2. b. pronounce
3. a. candid
4. d. exploration
5. b. sleeve
6. b. classical
7. a. cell
8. c. king
9. d. canine
10. b. satellite
11. a. book
12. c. Sahara
13. b. rust
14. d. tears
15. a. infinite
16. c. zeppelin

Lesson 9
1. b. web
2. d. today
3. a. FAX
4. d. Pacific
5. b. Africa
6. d. rock
7. a. prison
8. c. ear
9. b. second
10. d. building
11. a. hospital
12. b. QR
13. c. leading lady
14. d. senior
15. c. flower

Lesson 10
1. c. lake
2. d. steam
3. b. diamond
4. c. bird
5. a. island
6. d. unpretentious
7. b. statue
8. a. scurry
9. c. sigh
10. b. billion
11. a. river
12. d. classroom
13. c. law
14. b. labyrinth
15. a. whisper

Lesson 11
1. a. festival
2. c. bubble
3. b. yacht
4. d. valley
5. a. house
6. a. flour
7. b. sight
8. d. land
9. b. cry
10. c. year
11. a. craftsman
12. a. court
13. d. art
14. c. television
15. b. North America

Lesson 12
1. d. legislate
2. c. best
3. a. light
4. c. atmospheric pressure
5. d. wind
6. a. idiot
7. b. waltzes
8. d. temperature
9. c. skies
10. b. earth movement
11. a. goose
12. c. women
13. a. American
14. d. oases
15. b. gallon

Lesson 13
1. d. fungi
2. b. 65
3. d. viewing
4. c. knight
5. a. male
6. a. 21
7. c. plants
8. a. microorganism
9. b. 169
10. d. investigate
11. a. 50
12. c. live
13. b. respiration
14. a. 1/8
15. a. head

Lesson 14
1. a. time
2. b. $28y^3$
3. d. don't
4. c. land
5. b. play
6. d. biting
7. a. went
8. a. 6
9. b. sound
10. c. authorize
11. d. machinery
12. d. deer
13. b. 180
14. d. longest
15. c. distance

Lesson 15
1. c. gold
2. d. octopi
3. c. torrid
4. a. barbarous
5. c. rink
6. d. 3/2
7. c. capacity
8. b. humans
9. a. tree
10. b. aunt
11. d. cafeteria
12. d. does
13. a. monastery
14. c. melodious
15. d. battle
16. a. 29
17. c. parent
18. b. knot

Lesson 16
1. b. infancy
2. a. .26
3. d. easy
4. c. ounce
5. b. scrutinize
6. a. desert
7. d. principal
8. c. monologue
9. b. stick
10. a. dekaliter
11. d. printer
12. a. binary
13. c. infant
14. b. pure
15. d. ecstasy

Lesson 17
1. c. bucolic
2. a. steamship
3. d. ford
4. b. pots
5. c. dissolving
6. a. is
7. d. inch
8. d. metamorphic
9. b. sanctuary
10. a. villain
11. c. terrestrial
12. d. Mexico
13. b. zero
14. c. weep
15. a. mesmerize
16. d. squalor
17. b. India
18. c. convection

Lesson 18
1. b. pair
2. d. 64
3. c. novel
4. a. cooperative
5. b. plants
6. d. armory
7. c. audit
8. a. catacombs
9. d. cooling
10. b. peaceful
11. c. revival
12. d. companies
13. a. angles
14. b. candle
15. c. tactile
16. d. puzzle
17. d. blizzard
18. a. geometry

Lesson 19
1. c. rules
2. d. ethics
3. d. physical traits
4. b. voluntary
5. a. precipitation
6. c. lion
7. b. treaty
8. d. wind
9. a. vacillate
10. b. 1.35
11. c. avoid
12. a. ebullient
13. d. omnipotent
14. b. composition
15. a. scherzo
16. c. flawed
17. d. laser
18. b. plagiarist

Lesson 20
1. c. dome
2. a. holiday
3. d. theater
4. c. meter
5. c. metropolis
6. a. calendar
7. b. ecology
8. d. team
9. c. office
10. a. autocrat
11. d. water
12. b. hourglass
13. d. heat
14. a. parasite
15. c. education
16. b. homogeneous
17. a. Latin
18. c. chimera

Lesson 21
1. a. safety
2. d. attract
3. b. 100
4. c. tragedy
5. b. abstinence
6. a. backgammon
7. d. allegory
8. b. taught
9. d. light
10. a. philosophy
11. c. occasional
12. b. mirror
13. d. Mesozoic
14. a. communication
15. c. fortification
16. d. hexagon
17. b. aperture
18. c. linen

Lesson 22
1. c. museum
2. b. tame
3. d. hardness
4. a. fiftieth
5. b. tell
6. c. heat
7. d. acronym
8. b. cacti
9. a. tomb
10. c. glider
11. a. Scrooge
12. b. matter
13. d. Philippines
14. c. opportunity
15. a. flattery
16. d. artificial
17. a. ecstatic
18. d. exuberant

Lesson 23
1. c. moon
2. b. Aristotle
3. d. crops
4. b. yours
5. c. circle
6. a. -6
7. c. evangelist
8. d. French
9. b. laboratory
10. a. keyboard
11. a. commander
12. c. hibernation
13. d. education
14. b. car
15. a. authentic
16. c. filament
17. c. gustatory
18. d. octagon

Lesson 24
1. b. codes
2. c. obvious
3. d. Indian
4. a. granite
5. b. valor
6. a. China
7. c. commute
8. d. deterrent
9. b. zoologist
10. d. goose
11. c. algebra
12. a. cantankerous
13. b. sizzle
14. a. mundane
15. d. patient
16. c. archives
17. a. dictionary
18. c. rest

Lesson 25
1. d. cast
2. a. capital
3. c. emigrate
4. a. fleet
5. b. juvenile
6. d. companies
7. c. notorious
8. a. discomfort
9. b. 1 1/5
10. d. propaganda
11. c. ohms
12. a. minuscule
13. b. membrane
14. a. Hanukkah
15. d. microscope
16. c. commodities
17. c. Handel
18. d. Switzerland

Lesson 26
1. b. putrid
2. d. locate
3. d. Maya
4. a. rodent
5. b. polytheism
6. c. infection
7. d. ream
8. a. dove
9. b. rebellious
10. c. arithmetic
11. a. dock
12. d. complaints
13. b. criteria
14. a. .80
15. b. unremitting
16. c. oath
17. a. fencing
18. c. sterilize

Lesson 27
1. d. protect
2. c. pine
3. a. Nehru
4. b. advanced
5. c. scene
6. a. rain
7. b. hearing
8. d. manage
9. c. man's
10. a. sound
11. b. chain
12. d. saving
13. c. centimeter
14. a. campaign
15. b. country
16. d. sedative
17. a. music
18. b. diamond

Lesson 28
1. a. electorate
2. c. synthetic
3. d. thesaurus
4. b. guitar
5. a. crab
6. c. fusion
7. a. Antarctic
8. c. hew
9. d. lavender
10. b. aspirin
11. a. sedentary
12. c. profit
13. a. quartz crystal
14. c. Egypt
15. b. language
16. a. pass
17. c. arthritis
18. d. history

Common Core State Standards Alignment Sheet
Advancing Through Analogies

All lessons in this book align to the following standards.

Grade Level	Common Core State Standards
Grade 5 ELA-Literacy	L.5.5 Demonstrate understanding of figurative language, word relationships, and nuances in word meanings. L.5.6 Acquire and use accurately grade-appropriate general academic and domain-specific words and phrases, including those that signal contrast, addition, and other logical relationships (e.g., however, although, nevertheless, similarly, moreover, in addition).
Grade 6 ELA-Literacy	L.6.5 Demonstrate understanding of figurative language, word relationships, and nuances in word meanings. L.6.6 Acquire and use accurately grade-appropriate general academic and domain-specific words and phrases; gather vocabulary knowledge when considering a word or phrase important to comprehension or expression.
Grade 7 ELA-Literacy	L.7.5 Demonstrate understanding of figurative language, word relationships, and nuances in word meanings. L.7.6 Acquire and use accurately grade-appropriate general academic and domain-specific words and phrases; gather vocabulary knowledge when considering a word or phrase important to comprehension or expression.
Grade 8 ELA-Literacy	L.8.5 Demonstrate understanding of figurative language, word relationships, and nuances in word meanings. L.8.6 Acquire and use accurately grade-appropriate general academic and domain-specific words and phrases; gather vocabulary knowledge when considering a word or phrase important to comprehension or expression.